Buses, Coaches & Recolle
1967

Contents

Acknowledgments

Silver Link Publishing Ltd
The Trundle
Ringstead Road
Great Addington
Kettering
Northants NN14 4BW
Tel/Fax: 01536 330588
email: sales@nostalgiacollection.com
Website: www.nostalgiacollection.com

Apart from the three Crosville illustrations, all the remaining views in this book have come from the camera of Bob Gell; without these views and the detailed notes accompanying each slide this book would not have been possible. My most sincere thanks to Bob – outstanding!

The PSV Circle Fleet Histories for the operators featured in this book, together with a number of issues of *Buses Illustrated*, were vital sources of information.

© Henry Conn 2015
First published in 2015

ISBN 978 1 85794 446 4

British Library Cataloguing in Publication Data
A catalogue record for this book is available from the British Library.
Printed and bound in Ceská Republika

Frontispiece: **CALDAY GRANGE** This is Calday Grange, near West Kirby, Wirral, on 1 July 1967, and working service F34 is Crosville No SMG 400 (857 RFM), an ECW-bodied Bristol MW6G new in March 1961. This bus remained in the Crosville fleet until March 1979, being sold for scrap in July of that year.

BLACKPOOL Ribble operated services X60 and X70 between Manchester, Bolton, Chorley, Preston and Blackpool, and in the 1960s it was known as the world's most frequent express service. There was a scheduled departure every 15 minutes in the summer (with duplicates), and the most regular performers on this joint service were Ribble, North Western and Lancashire United. Standing in Blackpool bus station on 19 June 1967 is Ribble No 1782 (RCK 927), an MCW-bodied Leyland PD3/5 new in March 1962. Alongside is North Western No 172 (DDB 172C), an Alexander-bodied Daimler CRG6LX new in 1965

The Wimbledon Tennis Championships of 1 July 1967, shown on BBC2, marked the beginning of regular colour television in Britain, while A Whiter Shade of Pale by Procul Harum was No 1 on this day.

About the author

My first recollections of public transport were early in 1958 in my home town of Aberdeen, travelling from our home in Mastrick to Union Street, then onwards by tram to Bridge of Dee. My interest in buses, trolleybuses and trams expanded to taking fleet numbers or registration numbers, and by the mid-1960s I had acquired a camera and began my collection. This interest continued through my family's moves from Aberdeen to Perth, Whitburn in West Lothian, Banbury, Swindon and Oxford by 1974.

My first job was with Customs & Excise, beginning in London with transfers to Oxford,

Dover and Brighton. It was after I left Brighton that my enthusiasm for bus photography waned, and it never really returned apart from sporadic photography when I returned to Scotland in 1980. By this time I had left Customs & Excise and had returned to college in Cupar to study Agriculture. I met my future wife at this college and moved with her parents to Galloway, where I have lived very happily since 1983. To further my career I attended Aberdeen University to take a BSc Degree in Agriculture, and I successfully graduated in 1996. This led to me returning to the Civil Service with the Scottish Executive Rural Affairs Department, then through many changes to where I am now,

working with Natural England as adviser to farmers on Environmental Schemes (three days a week from last July).

By 2010 I had a significant collection of transport views from the mid-1960s to the early 1980s. I met with Silver Link Publishing's editor Will Adams in Preston in early 2010 and was very kindly given the opportunity to write a volume on Buses, Trams and Trolleybuses in the Midlands. Since then I have continued to enjoy writing volumes on transport for Silver Link, this volume being my first in the 'Recollections' series looking at buses, trolleybuses and trams as well as significant events in a specific year.

Introduction

This book is the third in the 'Recollections' series to look at bus and coach illustrations taken during a specific year, including the headline events that occurred either nationally or locally.

The year 1967 saw the UK enter the first round of negotiations for EEC membership in Rome; later Charles de Gaulle vetoed the UK's application – again. Jeremy Thorpe became leader of the Liberal Party, and Milton Keynes was formally designated by the Government as a new town, incorporating the nearby towns of Bletchley and Newport Pagnell. Parliament decided to nationalise 90% of the British steel industry, and the first North Sea gas was pumped ashore at Easington in the East Riding

of Yorkshire. The supertanker *Torrey Canyon* ran aground between Land's End and the Scilly Isles; a few days later the RAF bombed the ship and sank it. Car manufacturer Chrysler took full control of the Rootes Group, and Ford announced the end of the Anglia, replacing it with an all-new car to be called the Escort and built at Dagenham.

Puppet on a String, performed by Sandie Shaw, won the Eurovision Song Contest in 1967, and Desmond Morris's book *The Naked Ape* was published. Notable births in this year were Paul Gascoigne, Noel Gallagher, Jason Statham and Paul Ince.

All in colour, the illustrations start in Blackpool and journey south, visiting amongst other places

Liverpool, Sheffield, Crewe, Derby, Nottingham, Coventry, Cheltenham, Oxford and Newbury, then along the South Coast to visit Eastbourne, Brighton, Portsmouth, Southampton and Exeter to Torquay and Plymouth. Company or Corporation liveries featured include those of Ribble, Crosville, Derby and Nottingham Corporations, Midland Red, Black & White, Bristol, Stratford Blue, Devon General, Exeter Corporation, Hants & Dorset, Provincial, City of Oxford, Southdown, and the Corporations of Southampton, Portsmouth, Brighton and Eastbourne.

A number of independents are also featured, including Stevenson's, Hulley's, Green Bus, House of Watlington, Luxicoaches and Barton. Enjoy the nostalgia!

Photo	DESTINATIONS
1	**LIVERPOOL**
2	**DONCASTER**
3	**DONCASTER**
4	**DONCASTER**
5	**SHEFFIELD**
6	**SHEFFIELD**
7	**CHESTERFIELD**
8	**CHESTERFIELD**
9	**CHESTERFIELD**
10	**BAKEWELL**
11	**CREWE**
12	**UTTOXETER**
13	**UTTOXETER**
14	**DERBY**
15	**DERBY**
16	**DERBY**
17	**DERBY**

On 20 June the Monterey Pop Festival had taken place in California, the world's first large-scale outdoor rock music festival. Stars included the Who, Simon & Garfunkel, Eric Burdon & the Animals, the Byrds, Jefferson Airplane, Big Brother and the Holding Company with Janis Joplin and Jimi Hendrix.

LIVERPOOL Between July and October 1956 Liverpool took delivery of six Leyland PSU1/13s numbered SL171 to SL176 (SKB 168 to 173). They were fitted with Leyland 0.600 engines and bodies with a Crossley framework completed by Liverpool Corporation at Edge Lane. During 1961 SL171 to SL174 were reconstructed to C44F form by MCCW with raised rear compartments seating 20 over enlarged boots. At this time they were repainted in a livery of dark and light blue and were renumbered XL171 to XL174. They operated from Garston depot on the airport service until 1966, then on the summer service from Lime Street station to the Isle of Man ferry. Standing at the station on 19 June 1967 is No XL172 (SKB 169).

A few days after this photograph was taken, Ray Clemence was signed by Bill Shankly from Scunthorpe United for £18,000.

DONCASTER Hall Brothers of South Shields began with one coach in 1930, owned by Edward Hall and his brother Hubert. At the beginning they ran a service to Nottingham, later extended to Coventry. The service was created to enable miners and their families who had relocated to Coventry and North Warwickshire from the North East to visit friends and family in the Newcastle area. This is KCU 710, a Harrington-bodied AEC Reliance new to Hall Brothers in March 1964, photographed at Glasgow Paddocks in Doncaster on 27 December 1967. Now a car park, the area was used for long-distance coaches for many years during the 1950s and '60s. Hall Brothers' coaches were regular visitors, as were those of Barton Transport from Nottinghamshire. Both Hall Brothers and Taylor Brothers were taken over by Barton in July 1967.

Glasgow Paddocks, named after Lord Glasgow, a racehorse owner and breeder who stabled his horses here, was once the home of bloodstock auctioneers Tattersalls, who held sales on the site until 1957. Glasgow Paddocks was not just about horses, though, as the public space welcomed carnivals and galas. The bus station moved to part of Glasgow Paddocks before a purpose-built Southern bus station was built in 1968.

DONCASTER JFT 259, a Bedford VAL14 new to Taylor Brothers of South Shields in February 1964, was photographed at Glasgow Paddocks on the same day.

DONCASTER One of the last new coaches purchased by Taylor Brothers was CFT 203D, a Duple Northern-bodied Ford R192 new in June 1966. It is also seen at Glasgow Paddocks on 27 December 1967.

The ABC cinema in Doncaster opened on 18 May 1967 with Omar Sharif in Doctor Zhivago presented in 70mm. The cinema was a replacement for the Picture House, which had opened in 1914.

SHEFFIELD Joint Omnibus Committee was set up in 1929, its partners being the LNER, LMS and Sheffield Corporation. The fleet was split into three, A, B and C, and the buses carried a small blue letter showing the fleet allocation; if buses were used on the 'wrong' route, a cash transfer was made for the loan. The A fleet was used totally within the city boundary, the B fleet worked just outside the city boundary, and the C fleet handled long-distance services, which included Bakewell, Leeds and Manchester. The A fleet was owned totally by the Corporation, the B fleet was 50/50 between the Corporation and the railway companies, and the C fleet was totally owned by the railway companies, and passed to British Railways after nationalisation. At Pond Street bus station on 27 December 1967 is Roe-bodied AEC Regent III No 1744 (VWJ 544), new in March 1956; note that the fleet letter, above the offside headlamp, is 'B'.

On 11 December Concorde was unveiled at Toulouse in France.

SHEFFIELD Also seen on 27 December at Pond Street is Rotherham No 90 (5590 ET), one of three Roe-bodied AEC Renowns new in December 1964. The shell of these Renowns was built by Park Royal, and Roe completed the bodywork. After withdrawal by Rotherham, No 90 was noted with Bedlington & District in 1978.

*The Beatles film **Magical Mystery Tour** was premiered on BBC Television on 26 December.*

CHESTERFIELD In December 1963 Chesterfield took delivery of eight Park Royal-bodied AEC Reliances, Nos 23 to 30 (9023 to 9030 R). This is No 29 (9029 R) on 15 July 1967; it was withdrawn from service in July 1978 and sold for scrap in November.

On the day this photograph was taken Roberto De Vicenzo won the 96th Open Championship at Hoylake, his only major championship, two strokes ahead of defending champion Jack Nicklaus.

CHESTERFIELD Like a number of operators, Chesterfield was seduced by the charms of the Daimler Roadliner, but was quickly disillusioned by its unreliability. Ten Neepsend-bodied Daimler SRC6s were delivered between February and May 1967, numbered 71 to 80 (ORA 71E to 80E). This is No 80 on 15 July 1967, a little over two months into its service life. All ten had been withdrawn from service by October 1977; No 80 was the first to go, in January 1976, and was cannibalised for spares.

*The No 1 LP album on this day was **Sergeant Pepper's Lonely Hearts Club Band** by the Beatles.*

CHESTERFIELD By the early 1960s Hulley's passenger numbers were falling, so one-person, underfloor-engine buses were acquired; in 1963 an unusual purchase was a batch of S-type single-deckers built by Midland Red. These were followed by Leyland Royal Tigers from Yorkshire Traction, and

no fewer than ten Leyland Leopards from Sheffield Corporation. Hulley's buses could always be found on a stand immediately above the East Midland bus station in Chesterfield. The company's services were timed to reach Chesterfield at roughly 45 minutes past each hour, allowing a half-hour layover for the driver to try Kirk's sandwiches.

About to depart to Tideswell on 15 July 1967 is former Yorkshire Traction No 919 (DHE 350), a Brush-bodied Leyland PSU1/9 new in 1950. Production of the white Skoda 1100 in the right background had only begun in 1967.

BAKEWELL This is Rutland Square in Bakewell on the same day, and nearest the camera is Hulley's RC 9673, the former Trent No 767, a Willowbrook-bodied AEC Regal new in 1947. It was purchased by Hulley's in 1960, and lasted in the fleet until 1969. The Silver Service (Darley Dale) bus behind is DRB 10C, a Strachan Pacesaver-bodied Bedford SB, new in 1965.

Bakewell railway station closed to passengers a few months before the date of this view, on 6 March 1967.

CREWE Between late 1951 and early 1952 the last half-cab single-deck buses were delivered to Crosville; originally numbered KW 269 to 293, they were reclassified in May 1958 as SLB 270 to 293. This is SLB 275 (NFM 31), an ECW-bodied Bristol LWL6B working local Crewe service K14 to Sydney on 14 July 1967. SLB 275, 289 and 290 were the last half-cab single-deckers to remain in service with Crosville, 275 and 289 being withdrawn in January 1970, while 290 was sold in September of that year.

On this day Tommy Simpson, the British cyclist, died after collapsing during a mountain stage of the Tour de France in intense heat on the ascent of Mont Ventoux, a barren mountain rising over 6,000 feet near Carpentras.

CREWE Also working a local service, K43, in Crewe on 14 July is No DFG 65 (875 VFM), an ECW-bodied Bristol FSF6G new in January 1962. On delivery this bus was fitted with Cave-Brown-Cave heating, fluorescent lighting and illuminated offside advertisement panels. It remained in the Crosville fleet until it was sold to a dealer in March 1979.

On this day the Who begin a US tour, opening for Herman's Hermits.

UTTOXETER Standing in the Uttoxeter depot of the Green Bus Company on 8 July 1967 is No 38 (MAC 570), an all-Leyland PD2/12. This bus was new to Stratford-upon-Avon Blue Motors as its No 23 in 1952, and was withdrawn and sold to Green Bus in 1965.

*New films released on this day in 1967 were **The Dirty Dozen** and **You Only Live Twice.***

Below: **DERBY** At Derby bus station on 1 July 1967, on hire to Trent and working route 2 to Belper, is the Corporation's No 26 (ACH 626), one of six Brush-bodied Daimler CVD6s new in late 1947. No 26 remained in the Corporation fleet until 1968 and was sold for scrap in September of that year. In the background is Trent No 622 (622 CCH), a Northern Counties-bodied Daimler CRG6LX new in 1963.

*Today saw the first showing of **The Golden Shot**, hosted by Bob Monkhouse – do you remember 'Bernie the Bolt'?*

Above: **UTTOXETER** Southampton Corporation took delivery of five Park Royal-bodied Guy Arab UFs between June and August 1952, and another, 248, which arrived in February 1953; all six were originally fitted with dual doors. During 1955 they were all rebuilt to front entrance only, and re-seated to 36. After only 11 years of service, all were withdrawn and sold to North of Sherburn in December 1964.

Green Bus purchased five of them (JOW 917 to 920 and JOW 922), and they all entered service with 39 seats. This is Green Bus No 18 (JOW 918), which entered service in May 1965 and remained with the company until August 1970. Next in line is BSD 294, an NCME-bodied Daimler CVG6, which was new to Western SMT in 1948 and acquired by Green Bus in 1965. This view was taken at Uttoxeter depot on 8 July 1967.

*On this day the actress Vivien Leigh (who starred in **Gone with the Wind**) died in London at the tender age of 53.*

Below: **DERBY** In May 1962 Yorkshire Traction took delivery of three Willowbrook dual-purpose-bodied Leyland PSU3/3Rs, numbered 1230 to 1232 (XHE 230 to 232). They were renumbered 200 to 202 in April 1967, and sporting its new fleet number at Derby bus station on 8 July 1967 is No 202 (XHE 232). In May 1969 all three were converted to B53F form with roof-mounted destination boxes. No 202 was withdrawn from service in 1976 and sold for scrap in November of the following year.

Above: **DERBY** Working route 24 at Henley Green on 3 September 1967 is Derby Corporation No 107 (CRC 907), a Brush-bodied Foden PVD6 6LW that had been delivered as one of a batch of five in January 1952. The Fodens were well built, but were heavy and ponderous, and once the Roe-bodied Daimler CVG6s arrived in quantity the Fodens were generally used only at rush hours or for works services. Although non-standard, they still had long service lives, and No 107 remained in the fleet until 1969, being sold for scrap in July of that year.

At No 1 in the single charts on this day was **The Last Waltz,** *sung by Engelbert Humperdinck.*

DERBY On hire to Trent from Potteries Motor Traction, and departing from Derby bus station for Skegness on the same day as the previous picture, is No C8761 (761 CVT), a Willowbrook coach-bodied AEC Reliance new in March 1958. This bus was renumbered 761 in April 1972 and fitted for one-person operation, with jack-knife doors and painted in bus livery; it was withdrawn from service in April 1974, and via various routes and reconstructions it became a mobile café in April 1981.

Photo	DESTINATIONS
18	**NOTTINGHAM**
19	**NOTTINGHAM**
20	**NOTTINGHAM**
21	**NOTTINGHAM**
22	**NOTTINGHAM**
23	**BURTON-UPON-TRENT**
24	**BURTON-UPON-TRENT**
25	**BURTON-UPON-TRENT**
26	**BURTON-UPON-TRENT**
27	**COVENTRY**

NOTTINGHAM On Saturday 10 June 1967, departing from Huntingdon Street bus station in Nottingham for East Bridgford, is Skills No 60 (FRC 951), an all-Leyland PD2/12 new to Trent in January 1955 – this service was operated jointly with Trent! No 60 was purchased by Skills in May 1967 and was operated for a short period before being purchased by Trent for spares in September 1968.

On this day Israel, Syria, Jordan, Iraq and Egypt ended the 'Six Day War' with UN help.

NOTTINGHAM Working route 14 in Station Street on 15 August 1967 is West Bridgford No 5 (KAL 684), a Park Royal-bodied AEC Regent III new in February 1949. This bus passed to Nottingham City Transport in September 1968 as No 170 and was sold for scrap six months later.

Playing the Marquee in London on this day was Fleetwood Mac; the band members at this time were Peter Green (guitar, vocals), Mick Fleetwood (drums), Jeremy Spencer (guitar) and Bob Brunning (bass).

1967
No 1 Records

January
Green Green Grass of Home   Tom Jones
I'm a Believer   Monkees
February
This is my Song   Petula Clark
March
Release Me   Englebert Humperdinck
April
Somethin' Stupid   Frank Sinatra &
                                              Nancy Sinatra
Puppet on a String   Sandie Shaw
May
Silence is Golden   Tremeloes
June
A Whiter Shade of Pale   Procul Harum
July
All You Need is Love   Beatles
August
San Francisco   Scott Mckenzie
September
The Last Waltz   Englebert Humperdinck
October
Massachusetts   Bee Gees
November
Baby Now That I've Found You   Foundations
Let The Heartaches Begin   Long John Baldry
December
Hello Goodbye   Beatles

Left: **NOTTINGHAM** This is Upper Parliament Street on 3 September 1967, and working route 39 is No 496 (JTV 496E), a Metro-Cammell Weymann-bodied Leyland PDR1/2 new in January 1967. It was converted to dual doorway in September 1970, but unfortunately was destroyed by a fire at Parliament Street depot in December 1977.

On this day, Nottingham's Victoria railway station was closed.

Right: **NOTTINGHAM** Arnold is a market town and suburb of Nottingham, and working route 69 to Arnold from Long Row on Sunday 3 September 1967 is Nottingham No 234 (UTV 234), a Park Royal-bodied AEC Regent V new in March 1956. This bus was withdrawn from service in late 1971 and sold for scrap in March of the following year.

Sweden changed from driving on the left to driving on the right on this day. All non-essential traffic was banned from the roads from 01.00 to 06.00, and any vehicles on the road during that time had to follow special rules. All vehicles had to come to a complete stop at 04.50, then carefully change to the right-hand side of the road and stop again before being allowed to proceed at 05.00.

NOTTINGHAM

Beginning to show its age is Barton No 465 (HVO 133), a Duple-bodied Leyland PD1 new in 1948. This view was taken at Broad Marsh bus station on 30 December 1967. On the left, No 751 (135 BMV) is a Duple-bodied AEC Reliance new in 1954, which was purchased by Barton from Parlane of Aldershot in 1955.

In December 1967 it was a really good time to go to the movies, with new releases including **The Good, The Bad and The Ugly** *and* **The Graduate.**

BURTON-UPON-TRENT Between February and April 1953 Burton purchased from North in Leeds six Guy Arab II 5LWs (HGC 103, 118, 125, 130, 194 and 213), which had been delivered new to the London Passenger Transport Board. All six were reconditioned by Roe prior to entry into service. This is Burton No 70 (HGC 130), a Park Royal-bodied Guy Arab II that entered service in November 1953 and was withdrawn in January 1967. This view was taken at Horninglow Road depot on 8 July 1967, a few days before the bus was purchased for preservation.

On this day Billie Jean King beat Ann Jones to win the Ladies Singles championship at Wimbledon.

BURTON-UPON-TRENT Three Massey-bodied Guy Arab IVs were delivered to Burton in January 1959, numbered 73 to 75 (HFA 573 to 575). Also standing in Horninglow Road depot on the same day is No 74 (HFA 574), which was the last of the batch to be withdrawn in April 1972; all three passed to Tiger of Salsburgh the following month.

A few days before this picture was taken the first automatic cash machine was installed in the office of Barclays Bank in Enfield.

BURTON-UPON-TRENT The Leyland Royal Tiger PSU1 on the home market was among the most powerful and quiet buses, and was very smooth-riding, but from the outset the vacuum brakes were not as efficient or as responsive as drivers desired. The home-market bus also lacked the air-servo assistance to the clutch or gear change that the overseas PSUs possessed, and as a result clutch pressures were heavy, gear-lever throws rather long, and the unassisted steering hard to move at low road speeds. Drivers of the Royal Tiger regarded the type as hard work, though rewarding, to drive, and some operators swore by the model – while others swore at it. This is Stevenson's No 7 (DHE 352), a Brush-bodied Leyland PSU1/9 new to Yorkshire Traction in 1951; it is seen at Wetmore Road bus park in Burton on 8 July 1967.

BURTON-UPON-TRENT This is Stevenson's No 30 (EHE 160), another Leyland Royal Tiger, this time variant PSU1/13, which was 8 feet wide rather than the PSU1/9's 7ft 6in. No 30 had also been new to Yorkshire Traction in 1952 and had Roe bodywork, which was a little less harsh than the Brush-bodied vehicle in the previous view, taken on the same day and at the same location.

COVENTRY The BMMO CM6 and CM6T production vehicles were completely restyled from the prototype, with a new six-bay body format that BMMO subsequently copied on all future designs. BMMO constructed 29 examples at its Central Works, and they entered service between February 1965 and May 1966. Twenty-four were built as CM6Ts with 44 seats and a rear toilet, while the remaining five, fleet numbers 5667-71, were built as CM6s without a toilet and with 46 seats. The engine was a 10½-litre naturally aspirated BMMO KL, driving through an SCG five-speed semi-automatic gearbox, making the CM6 type unique as the only BMMO-designed vehicle fitted with this type of gearbox. The brakes were discs front and rear with a continuous charging system for the servo. This is CM6T No 5663 (DHA 963C), which entered service from Nuneaton in December 1965. The bus was repainted with a maroon roof in June 1967 and this picture, at Pool Meadow in Coventry, was taken on 20 August 1967; it will be working a Coventry to London express service. No 5663 was withdrawn from service in April 1974 and, via Catteralls of Southam, Morris of Pencoed and Evertons of Droitwich, was broken up for spares in June 1976, with the engine passing to Worcester Bus Preservation Society.

*The film **Bonnie and Clyde** opened this week in August 1967, and the No 1 single was **San Francisco (Be Sure To Wear Some Flowers in Your Hair)** sung by Scott McKenzie.*

CHELTENHAM COACH STATION During the 1960s and '70s Cheltenham was renowned for the mass exodus of coaches at 2pm on a Saturday afternoon – as many as 200 coaches would depart at the same time for destinations countrywide. Departing from Cheltenham Coach Station for Paignton on 20 August 1967 is Ribble No 792 (ARN 792C), a Plaxton-bodied Leyland PSU3/3RT new in April 1965.

The average house price in the UK in August 1967 was £3,840, and the average weekly wage was £21 7s 0d.

CHELTENHAM COACH STATION
had a refuelling area consisting of a covered through building with two pits and three roads, where refuelling and routine servicing of Black & White coaches took place between journeys. Located at the side of this building was a drive-through vehicle wash, and making use of this facility on 20 August 1967 is Black & White No 251 (AAD 251B), a Harrington Cavalier-bodied AEC Reliance new in 1964.

In August 1967 a half loaf (pan) was 1s 9d, and a half loaf (plain) was 1s 6d.

CHELTENHAM COACH STATION The rush to leave the Coach Station is on, and leading the pack on 3 July 1967 is Hants & Dorset No 894 (AEL 2B), an ECW-bodied Bristol MW6G new in April 1964. The bodywork featured sliding side vents, which opened from the centre, jack-knife entrance doors and three-way opening roof ventilators; No 894 also had air suspension and air/hydraulic brakes. This bus was taken out of service in October 1975 and is now in preservation. On the left, heading for Yarmouth, is Eastern Counties No RE880 (GNG 92C), an ECW-bodied Bristol RELH6G new in 1965.

CHELTENHAM COACH STATION

With the kind assistance of a traffic warden, No 212 (4212 AD) is heading for Birmingham on the same day, closely followed by No 214 (4214 AD), both Plaxton-bodied AEC Reliances new in 1960.

News at Ten premiered on British TV on this day.

CHELTENHAM COACH STATION

This is 4847 R, a Bedford SB5 bodied by Yeates and new to Parkin (Luxicoaches) of Borrowash, Derby. This picture was also taken on 3 July 1967.

On this day John Wayne fans would have been going to the cinema to see El Dorado.

CHELTENHAM The first four bus-bodied Bristol REs delivered to the Bristol Omnibus Co were allocated to its Cheltenham District subsidiary. This is one of the four, No 1001 (KHW 307E), working route 587 to Cleeve Hill on 20 August 1967; it was later transferred to Staple Hill depot in Bristol, and all four were converted to dual-door layout.

If you went to the cinema on this day you could have been watching **Point Blank** *with Lee Marvin or* **In the Heat of the Night** *with Sidney Poitier.*

GLOUCESTER Bristol Omnibus route 529 was a long-standing hourly service from Cheltenham to Bristol via Gloucester. Standing at the Royal Wells bus station in Gloucester on 20 August 1967 is Bristol No L8455 (YHT 955), an ECW-bodied Bristol LD6G new in November 1957. After a long service life, the bus was withdrawn in 1976 and sold for scrap in October of that year.

A few days earlier the Small Faces had been in concert at Cheltenham Town Hall.

GLOUCESTER This is Stratford Blue No 51 (5451 WD), one of five Marshall-bodied Leyland PSUC1/1s that were new in 1962. It is about to work route 64A to Evesham on 20 August 1967.

In August 1967 a gallon of petrol cost 5s 2d (27p), and you could buy a new Ford Cortina Mark II for £749.

GLOUCESTER
Working route X73
between Birmingham
and Cheltenham on the
same day is Midland
Red No 5177 (5177
HA), a Willowbrook
dual-purpose-bodied
Leyland PSU3/4R new
in April 1963 and
allocated to Digbeth
depot in Birmingham.
In November 1968 No
5177 was fitted for
one-person operation,
and in May 1971 was
re-seated with bus
seats. On the transfer
of Midland Red services
in the West Midlands,
this bus moved to the
West Midlands Passenger
Transport Executive on
3 December 1973 and
remained in that fleet
until March 1978.

*The fantastic song
Light my Fire by the
Doors was in the UK
charts throughout
August 1967.*

OXFORD In March 1960 Provincial of Leicester purchased a Duple Britannia-bodied AEC Reliance. Later this bus, XBC 546, was purchased by Barton and given fleet number 1055, and this picture was taken at Peartree Services off the A34 north of Oxford on 22 July 1967. This bus passed to Llynfi Motors of Maesteg in 1974.

Peartree Services were opened by Forte on 29 June 1964, and built alongside in 1967 was the Excelsior Motor Lodge.

OXFORD Standing at Gloucester Green bus station on 17 September 1967 is No 325, a Park Royal-bodied AEC Bridgemaster. The last of these buses purchased new by City of Oxford arrived in 1962, and were numbered 316 to 328 (316 to 328 NJO); they were the only short-length front-entrance Bridgemasters built. No 725 was acquired by Premier in March 1973, but for spares only.

Three days after this picture was taken the Queen Elizabeth 2 was launched at Clydebank.

WATLINGTON

Dutfield Motors was established in September 1947 at Portsmouth Road, Godalming, and by July 1948 was building a coach each week, inspired by Duple designs of the period. The company lasted in its original form until 1950, when it merged with Longford Coachworks of Neath. It built a 32-seat coach for House of Watlington on a Commer Avenger chassis, and EBW 806 is seen here on 17 September 1967. Behind is DUD 810, a Duple Vista-bodied Bedford OB bought new by House, while on the left is Harrington-bodied Bedford SB8 WXC 347, new to Ewer in May 1959 and purchased second-hand by the company.

On this day **Mission Impossible** *premiered on American TV.*

WALLINGFORD New to Sheffield United Tours in 1955 was this Duple Elizabethan-bodied AEC Reliance, TWJ 247. This view was taken at the depot of Tappin's of Wallingford on 17 September 1967.

On this day, Jim Morrison and the Doors famously defied CBS censors on **The Ed Sullivan Show** *when they performed* **Light My Fire.**

1967 Happenings (1)

January
> Jeremy Thorpe becomes leader of the Liberal Party.
> Milton Keynes designated as a 'new town'

February
> British submarine HMS Renown launched

March
> Queen Elizabeth Hall opened in London
> First North Sea Gas pumped ashore in Yorkshire
> Super-tanker *Torrey Canyon* runs aground off Land's End - later bombed by RAF and sunk

April
> UK wins Eurovision Song Contest with *Puppet on a String* sung by Sandie Shaw
> Expo 67 World Trade Fair opens in Canada, marking 100th anniversary of British North America Act, 1867

May
> UK applies for membership of EEC

June
> Six-Day War - Israel occupies West Bank, Gaza Strip, Sinai Peninsula and Golan Heights
> Barclays Bank installs first automatic cash machine in Enfield, England

NEWBURY About to work the 6-mile journey from Newbury bus station to East Woodhay on 29 July 1967 is S319 (TWL 59), an ECW coach-bodied Bristol LS6B new in 1953 as No 94 in the fleet of Thames Valley (to be operated by South Midland). On the right, No 743 (JRX 818) is an ECW-bodied Bristol KSW6B new in 1955.

The International Love-in Festival took place at Alexandra Palace on this day, featuring among others Pink Floyd and the Animals.

EASTBOURNE The first diesel-engined
buses delivered to Eastbourne were six
East Lancashire-bodied Leyland PD1s, which arrived in October 1946, apart
from one that was delivered in May 1947. Five of the six were rebuilt to
open-top form, and this 27 July 1967 view shows No 13 (JK 9111), which was
converted in late 1961. It was withdrawn from service in February 1968 and
sold that year to the Royal Coach Inn, Houston, Texas.

*A couple of months after the date of this picture the Moody
Blues played at the Catacombs in Eastbourne.*

EASTBOURNE Between March and April 1966 Eastbourne took delivery of ten East Lancashire-bodied Leyland PD2A/30s, Nos 71 to 80 (BJK 671D to 680D), and all had entered service by May. This is No 71 (BJK 671D) on 27 July 1967. After just over 15 years in the fleet No 71 was withdrawn during August 1981 and passed into preservation.

In the early hours of 23 July 1967 one of the worst riots in US history broke out on 12th Street, Detroit. By the time the riot was quelled on the 27th, having involved 7,000 National Guard and US army troops, 43 people had died, nearly 1,200 had been injured and nearly 1,400 buildings had been burned.

1967 Happenings (2)

July

First colour television broadcasts begin on BBC 2 (full colour service commenced on BBC 2 from 2 December)

Decriminalisation of homosexuality in England

Steam traction eliminated on Southern Region of British Rail

August

Marine Broadcasting Offences Act outlaws pirate radio stations

September

RMS *Queen Mary* makes her final transatlantic voyage

BBC introduces Radio 1, Radio 2, Radio 3 and Radio 4

October

Abortion legalised in defined circumstances

Charles De Gaulle vetoes British entry into EEC

November

Hither Green rail crash

BBC opens first local radio station in Leicester

£ sterling devalued from $2.80 to $2.40

December

World's first heart transplant operation carried out by Christiaan Barnard in Cape Town, South Africa

Right: **BRIGHTON** From 1962 until 1965 Brighton, Hove & District reverted to the use of the open rear-entrance Bristol with the delivery of Nos 41 to 72. These differed from the earlier FS type in having a revised grille. As with the Bristol FSFs, alternate batches had either Bristol BVW or Gardner 6LW engines. Nos 41 to 44 were convertible open-toppers, while Nos 45 to 50 were closed-top and featured offside illuminated advertisement panels. 1963 saw further closed-top arrivals, Nos 55 to 57, followed by convertibles Nos 51 to 54 in 1964. From No 51 onwards the Cave-Brown-Cave heating system was reintroduced (a feature on all subsequent new BH&D Lodekkas), while Nos 53 and 54 differed from the rest of the convertible fleet in that they were painted red and cream as opposed to all-over cream, this pair being used on a new circular tour service. Working that service on Brighton seafront on 26 July 1967 is No 54 (APN 54B).

EASTBOURNE Between March and June 1964 Southdown took delivery of 25 NCME-bodied Leyland PD3/4s, Nos 400 to 424 (400 to 424 DCD). All were convertible to open-top form, the roof being removed and replaced with handrails and Perspex screens. Representing this batch is No 409 (409 DCD), seen here working the route from Eastbourne Parade to Beachy Head on 27 July 1967.

The Brighton Fringe, created in 1967, is an open-access mixed arts event, which means that it does not book performers, but is approached by people wishing to be part of the Fringe – anyone can put on an event. Participants vary from complete beginners to hardened professional shows, and everything in between.

BRIGHTON Corporation took delivery of eight Weymann bodied AEC Regent IIIs in June 1947, numbered 81 to 88 (HUF 81 to 88), and all entered service in August of that year. This is No 88 (HUF 88) at the Old Steine on 26 July 1967. It was one of the last of the batch to be withdrawn in June 1968 after 21 years of sterling service, and was sold to Cooper of Ringmer for scrap in December 1968.

In concert at Brighton Dome a few months later were Jimi Hendrix, the Move, Pink Floyd, Amen Corner and the Nice. Tickets were 7s 6d, 10s 6d, 12s 6d and 15 shillings!

BRIGHTON Twenty MCW Orion-bodied Leyland PD2/37s were delivered to Brighton Corporation during 1959. This is No 74 (WCD 74), which entered service on 25 March of that year; it is on the Old Steine, working route 53 between there and Hollingdean. By February 1971 the bus was being used mainly for driver training and relief duties, and by June of that year had become the permanent driver trainer bus.

Brickwoods Best Bitter was brewed in Portsmouth, but the company was sold to Whitbread in 1971; bottling ceased at its base in Portsea ten years later and the brewery was closed for good in 1983.

1967
Arrivals & Departures

Births

Mark Lamarr	TV and Radio presenter	7 January
Dale Gordon	Footballer	29 January
Tamsin Greig	Actress	23 February
Jonathan Firth	Actor	6 April
Noel Gallagher	Musician	29 May
Nicole Kidman	Actress	20 June
Pamela Anderson	Actress	1 July
Tara Fitzgerald	Actress	18 September
Davina McCall	Actress	16 October
Julia Roberts	Actress	28 October
Gavin Rossdale	Musician	30 October
Letitia Dean	Actress	14 November

Deaths

Ann Sheriden	Actress	(b.1915)	21 January
Victor Gollancz	Publisher	(b.1893)	8 February
Nelson Eddy	Musician	(b.1901)	6 March
Konrad Adenauer	Chancellor of Germany	(b.1876)	19 April
John Masefield	Poet	(b.1878)	12 May
Spencer Tracy	Actor	(b.1900)	10 June
Jayne Mansfield	Actress	(b.1933)	29 June
Vivien Leigh	Actress	(b.1913)	8 July
Joe Orton	Playwright	(b.1933)	9 August
Siegfried Sassoon	Poet	(b.1886)	1 September
Sir Malcolm Sargent	Musician	(b.1895)	3 October
Woody Guthrie	Musician	(b.1912)	3 October
Clement Attlee	UK Prime Minister	(b.1883)	8 October
Sydney Barnes	Cricketer	(b.1873)	26 December
Paul Whiteman	Musician	(b.1890)	29 December

BRIGHTON Standing in the rather cramped Pool Valley bus station on 26 July 1967 is Southdown No 642 (OUF 642), a Park Royal-bodied Leyland PSUC1/1 new in June 1955. This bus had a long service life, being withdrawn from the fleet in early 1971 and sold by April; in February 1973 it was bought by civil engineering contractor McAlpine as a workers' bus. Beyond No 642 is No 315 (GUF 250D), the Northern Counties-bodied Leyland PD3/4 that was exhibited at the 1966 Commercial Motor Show and had an experimental heating and ventilating system.

BRIGHTON On the same day in Pool Valley bus station, and indicating a journey to Cowfold, is No 164 (HUF 764E), a Marshall-bodied Leyland PSU3/3RT that had entered service only a few weeks earlier.

PORTSMOUTH Working route 26 to Hayling Ferry from Eastney on 23 July 1967 is Portsmouth No 60 (GTP 977), an all-Leyland PD2/10 new in 1952.

A few months earlier the Who played a gig at the Birdcage in Eastney Road, while in mid-summer the Guildhall offered Acker Bilk, and the King's Theatre featured Engelbert Humperdinck for one week.

Left: **PORTSMOUTH** Intended initially for long-distance private hire and excursion work, three ECW-bodied Bristol MW6Gs, Nos 715 to 717 (673 to 675 AAM), were delivered to Wilts & Dorset in May 1962 and entered service a month later. A new livery of cream with a red waistband was introduced at this time. The buses were upholstered in grey hide and grey with green moquette, and were provided with gangway carpets. They were the first buses delivered to the company with a public address system and fluorescent lighting. This is No 716 (674 AAM) in Hyde Park Road, Portsmouth, on 22 July 1967.

Below: **SOUTHSEA** In November 1966 Aldershot & District took delivery of five Metro-Cammell Weymann coach-bodied AEC Reliances, Nos 531 to 535 (FHO 531D to 535D). At the coach park in Southsea on 23 July 1967 is No 535.

A few months before this photograph was taken, on 4 March 1967, Hovertravel SR-N6 012 overturned off the Southsea terminal with the loss of five lives.

Above: **PORTSMOUTH** The transport hub at Portsmouth Harbour is known as The Hard, the name deriving from an area of foreshore that was sufficiently firm – naturally or man-made – to allow easy access to the boats moored along it. Between March and October 1967 Portsmouth took delivery of 26 Leyland PSRC1/1 Panthers, Nos 150 to 175; the first 12 were bodied by Marshall and the remainder by Metro-Cammell Weymann. Nearest the camera in this view from 28 July 1967 is No 154 (GTP 154E) with bodywork by Marshall, compared to No 162 (GTP 162E), bodied by MCW.

SOUTHSEA A large number of Beadle-bodied Leyland PSUC1/2s were purchased new by Southdown between February and July 1957. One of them was No 1092 (SUF 892), seen here at Southsea on the same day as the previous picture; it had been repainted in the blue livery of Triumph Coaches in March 1963, and was returned to Southdown livery in April 1968. It was with contractor Wimpey in August 1969, moving to McAlpine in May 1972.

SOUTHSEA Operating London Transport staff day trips from Wood Green and Plumstead depots to Southsea on 23 July 1967 are AEC Routemasters RM 925 (WLT 925) and RM 81 (VLT 81). The latter entered service from Poplar depot in November 1959 and remained with London Transport at various locations until February 1986, when it was purchased by Clydeside Scottish. In June 1992 it was purchased by East Yorkshire and remained there until December 1995, when it was converted to open-top form and exported to Madeira. RM 925 entered service on route 260 in January 1962 and remained with London Transport until April 1991, when it was sold for scrap.

SOUTHSEA In May 1964 Skills of Nottingham purchased new a Plaxton-bodied Bedford VAL14, No 50 (ATV 50B). By October 1966 Yeates of Loughborough had purchased the coach, selling it in March the following year to Campings Luxury Coaches of Brighton. It is seen here at Southsea in Campings' livery on 23 July 1967, but the company did not retain the coach for long; by the end of that month it had passed to Seaview Coaches of Parkstone.

Note the 1966-registered Morris 1100 Mark I on the right. The Mark II, with a 1,275cc engine, was announced at the end of May 1967 and was available from October.

GOSPORT Provincial took delivery of three Park Royal utility-bodied Guy Arab IIs in 1943, Nos 56 to 58 (EHO 868 to 870); they were painted grey and had wooden slatted seats. The body of No 56 was rebuilt to open-top form in 1958 and is seen here in Gosport, also on 23 July 1967. It was sold for scrap in April 1969. In the background is No 74 (GHO 595), a Guy Arab III that was rebuilt with Reading full-front bodywork and fitted with a Deutz air-cooled engine.

Photo	DESTINATIONS
57	**SOUTHAMPTON**
58	**SOUTHAMPTON**
59	**SOUTHAMPTON**
60	**SOTHAMPTON**
61	**EXETER**
62	**TORQUAY**
63	**TORQUAY**
64	**BRIXHAM**
65	**PLYMOUTH**

SOUTHAMPTON Delivered in March 1949, and entering service on the 6th, No 167 (FTR 514), a Guy Arab III with a Park Royal H30/26R body, was one of a large batch of tramway replacement vehicles, and together with many others it formed the very standardised Southampton Corporation Transport fleet of the 1950s. In May 1967 No 167 was converted to open-top form and is seen here on 25 July in its first season of service on tours of the city and docks.

Below: **SOUTHAMPTON** During May and June 1964 East Kent took delivery of 12 Duple-bodied AEC Reliances (AFN 488B to 499B). Standing in the parking area for the Isle of Wight ferry on 25 July 1967 is AFN 488B. It was withdrawn from service in early 1978, and by May of that year was noted in the fleet of Ebdon's Coaches of Sidcup.

In 1967 more than 273,000 cars and 24,000 buses and lorries used the Isle of Wight ferries.

Below left: **SOUTHAMPTON** This is Hants & Dorset FRU 827, photographed in Southampton on 25 July 1967. Entering service in May 1946, this Bristol K5G had ECW bodywork and was given the fleet number TD 782. This was changed to 1116 in January 1950, and in 1956 the bus was rebodied by ECW. Subsequently it was converted to a driver trainer, as seen here.

In July 1967 you could take the Seaspeed hovercraft from Southampton to Cowes for 15 shillings each way. There were 12 flights each weekday and the journey time was 20 minutes.

Below: **SOUTHAMPTON** Hants & Dorset took delivery of a large number of Bristol K6s in 1950. Also seen in Southampton on 25 July 1967 is one of them, No 1265 (KEL 708), which had ECW bodywork and was new in August 1950. In May 1955 the original bodywork was scrapped following a fire caused by overheated rear brakes. Compare the newer bodywork with that of No 1245 (JEL 264), standing on the right – No 1265 has a six-bay construction, a smoother profile and three-aperture indicators. This bus was sold to a dealer in September 1969 and acquired by Yates Tours of Runcorn in February 1970, where it remained until August 1972, when it was sold to a dealer in Bolton.

1967 saw the UK driver introduced to the Ford Escort Mark I.

EXETER Budleigh Salterton is a small town on the coast of East Devon, 15 miles south-east of Exeter, and heading there from Exeter bus station is Exeter Corporation No 175 (JFJ 875), a Weymann-bodied Daimler CVD6 new in 1950 – it is now preserved.

In Exeter in 1967, Norman & Pring (part of Whitbread) amalgamated with another Whitbread brewery, Starkey, Knight & Ford, and relocated to Tiverton – the City Brewery premises were put up for sale. In July of that year fire raged through the brewery, and 30-foot flames leapt through the roof. The fire service put the cause down to sparks from oxy-acetylene equipment that was being used to dismantle the vats.

EXETER In March 1967 Devon General took delivery of five Marshall-bodied AEC Reliances, Nos 40 to 44 (HOD 40E to 44E). This is No 42 (HOD 42E) at Exeter bus station on 12 June 1967. The bus in the background is No 842 (XTA 842), a Willowbrook-bodied Albion Nimbus, an unusual purchase by Devon General but ideal for some of the narrow roads in the area.

Also during 1967 the Head Weir Paper Mill, just below Blackaller Weir on the River Exe in Exeter, closed and was converted into a pub and restaurant.

Above: **TORQUAY** Working local route 34 at Castle Circus in Torquay on 11 June 1967 is Devon General No 971 (971 MDV), one of a batch of 16 Metro-Cammell-bodied AEC Regent Vs new in 1963.

Above right: **TORQUAY** During 1960 Devon General took delivery of 23 Roe-bodied Leyland PDR1/1s, and representing this batch is No 917 (917 DTT), seen here working route 31 at Castle Circus on the same day as the previous picture.

The day before these pictures were taken the Yardbirds featured at the Princess Theatre in Torquay, and a few days later Procul Harum appeared there.

Right: **BRIXHAM** On tour to this Devon fishing port, also on 11 June 1967, is Greenslade coach FFJ 14D, a Duple Northern-bodied AEC Reliance that was just one year old. It was purchased by Scarlet Coaches of Minehead in January 1976, then passed to Born's Coaches of Okehampton in September 1978, and was withdrawn for scrap in March 1979.

If you were in Brixham on 28 April 1967 a flying saucer was reported by several witnesses hovering for 80 minutes over the town at an altitude of 15,000 feet.

PLYMOUTH During June 1967 East Yorkshire took delivery of two Metro-Cammell Weymann-bodied Leyland PSUR1/2Rs, Nos 823 and 824 (JRH 323E and 324E). Standing in Bretonside bus station in Plymouth on 13 June 1967 is JRH 324E, in its first season of touring. Both buses were withdrawn in 1976 and passed to the National Bus Company cannibalisation centre at Bracebridge Heath in October of that year for spares.

A couple of weeks earlier, on 28 May, crowds of 250,000 turned out in Plymouth to welcome home Devon yachtsman Francis Chichester. Chichester had just sailed his yacht Gypsy Moth IV around the world in what was the first true circumnavigation via the three Capes of Hope, Leeuwin and Horn.

Index of Operators and Vehicles